GET IT YET?

EVERYDAY RULES FOR THE GAME OF LIFE

A. HUGH SCHINTZIUS, ED.B., M.ED.

Beth,
With Love,
Hugh

IUNIVERSE, INC.
NEW YORK   BLOOMINGTON

Get It Yet?
Everyday Rules for the Game of Life

The views expressed in this work are solely those of the author and do not necessarily reflect the views of the publisher, and the publisher hereby disclaims any responsibility for them.

iUniverse books may be ordered through booksellers or by contacting:

iUniverse
1663 Liberty Drive
Bloomington, IN 47403
www.iuniverse.com
1-800-Authors (1-800-288-4677)

Because of the dynamic nature of the Internet, any Web addresses or links contained in this book may have changed since publication and may no longer be valid.

ISBN: 978-1-4401-5952-7 (sc)
ISBN: 978-1-4401-5953-4 (dj)
ISBN: 978-1-4401-5954-1 (ebk)

Printed in the United States of America

iUniverse rev. date: 7/22/2009

To: _____

From: _____

Date: _____

To my Teachers

Dear Soul,
Live the simple wisdom that follows …
and you will create a life of joy
and prosperity for yourself.

CONTENTS

INTRODUCTION

I once read that there is a story behind every book. This introduction is my story of how what started out as a poster turned into a personal manuscript, and finally, after much encouragement from a couple hundred of my friends, colleagues, and students, ended up as a book.

As a university faculty administrator for thirty-three years, I realized very early in my career that I had a much larger influence upon my students than just the subject matter of what I was teaching in my classes and the example of how I conducted myself as an administrator.

In the mid-1990s, this book started out as a poster of eight guidelines as a way to live my life that I posted on a wall of my home library/reading/study/computer room.

I came upon those eight guidelines as a result of my reading, for over twenty years, ancient history, the early great philosophers, what many would categorize as the holy writings of the major religions, and my comparative study of fifteen versions of the Bibles that I had been researching and reading. Six of the guidelines I found in the various versions of the Bibles.

I wrote the eight guidelines on the poster, in large font, as "two-liners" as follows:

"What you sow …
is what you will reap."

"Do unto others …
as you would have others do unto you."

"As you judge …
you will be judged."

"As you forgive …
you will be forgiven."

"As you accuse …
you will be accused."

"As you condemn …
you will be condemned.

"What goes around …
comes around."

"Every action …
has an opposite and equal reaction."

After some weeks of looking at my poster, I had a eureka flashbulb kind of moment when I realized that judging, forgiving, condemning, and accusing were only interactions among people. Accepting as I did that those statements about judging, forgiving, accusing, and condemning were valid statements, because you reap what you sow, what goes around comes around, and for every action there is an opposite and equal reaction, I figured that I could take any and every interaction between people, make a "two-liner" out of it, and it had to be equally valid.

So, I began observing how people interacted with each other, positively and not so positively. With notebook and pen in my pocket, day by day, I would write down how I saw people treating each other and what they said to each other. At night at home, I'd make "two-liners" of what I had observed of peoples' interactions. It was after I had written over a hundred of these that I started looking at these "two-liners" as "rules" for this thing that I heard people referring to as "the game of life."

I printed out a few copies of what was becoming a manuscript. I then asked a handful of people if they would mind reading it and sharing their thoughts about it with me. Surprisingly to me, everyone who read the manuscript said I should publish it as a book.

I continued adding not only "two-liners" to the manuscript but some three-, four-, and five-liners as the interactions between people seemed to dictate. After several more months, I had a manuscript of over three hundred "rules." I again printed out a few copies and asked different people to read it and share their thoughts. This time I was told that I needed to publish it as a book because the message could be life transforming for many people. Some even suggested that the message could be world transforming. As one person said to me, "Imagine how beautiful life would be if everyone on Earth interacted with everyone else, truly believing that what they did for and to everyone else was going to come back to themselves, at some point in time, either to seemingly bless them or to painfully haunt them."

In 1997 I self-published the book and sold 140 copies. The feedback from the first sales was very encouraging, but as so often happens, events come along in our lives that result in things getting "put on the back burner." And so it was with this book at that time, mainly due to my responsibilities at the university.

After I retired in 2005, moved to a warmer climate, had a house built, got settled in, and re-energized, several of my university colleagues with whom I had remained in touch and who had read the manuscript years earlier began telling me to "get that book published!"

Well, I guess if enough people tell you to do something, "ya just gotta do it."

It is my sincere hope that this book has as great an impact upon your life, how you interact with people, the role model you become for everyone you cross paths with, and your future, as writing it has had upon my life. You can become a transformative agent by spreading this basic universal message.

The Rules contained in this book are ones that I have observed as I have watched people interact with each other. I recognize that there are many more Rules (interactions) between people that I have not included. In the last section, titled My Personal Rules, the reader is encouraged to write his/her own Rules based upon his/her own life story.

Peace, light, and much love to all.

A. Hugh Schintzius

GENERAL RULES

What goes around ...
comes around.

As you do to others ...
others will do to you.

What you sow ...
is what you will reap.

The result of every action ...
is an equal and opposite reaction.

As you judge …
you will be judged.

As you condemn …
you will be condemned.

As you accuse …
you will be accused.

An eye for an eye …
a tooth for a tooth.

What you plant …
is what you harvest.

Plant rice …
harvest rice.

Plant a cupful …
harvest several cupfuls.

Plant a bushelful …
harvest many bushelfuls.

Plant a little …
harvest a little.

Plant a lot …
harvest a lot.

Plant nothing …
harvest nothing.

Plant a variety …
harvest a variety.

The earlier in the season that you plant …
the earlier that you will harvest.

The earlier in your lifetime
that you do something for someone …
the earlier in your lifetime
that someone will do something for you.

Plant a weed …
gather many weeds.

Plant a green pepper seed …
harvest many green peppers.

Plant a yellow pepper seed …
harvest many yellow peppers.

Plant a red pepper seed …
harvest many red peppers.

LOVE

Plant a cherry tree seed ...
and, after some years ...
and for many years ...
gather many cherries.

Be loving toward someone ...
have someone be loving toward you.

Be loving toward many ...
have many be loving toward you.

As you forgive …
you will be forgiven.

Forgive many …
be forgiven by many.

Never forgive someone …
have someone never forgive you.

Do something for someone ...
have someone do something for you.

The more that you do for someone ...
the more that someone will do for you.

What you do to someone ...
someone will do to you.

Speak kindly of someone ...
have someone speak kindly of you.

Help someone in need …
have someone help you
when you are in need.

Help many who are in need …
be helped by many
in your times of need.

Assist someone …
be assisted by someone.

Make someone blissful …
have someone make you blissful.

Be a brother/sister to someone …
have someone be a brother/sister to you.

Be there for someone
in the time of their sorrow …
have someone be there
in the time of your sorrow.

Compliment someone …
be complimented by someone.

Be a sincere companion to someone …
have someone be a sincere companion to you.

Show compassion toward someone …
have someone show compassion toward you.

Be considerate toward someone …
have someone be considerate toward you.

Help an elderly person …
have someone help you
when you are elderly.

Comfort someone
who grieves the loss of a loved one …
be comforted by someone
when you grieve the loss of a loved one.

Flirt with someone
to get something you want from her/him ...
have someone flirt with you
to get something she/he wants from you.

Give someone a gift from your heart ...
have someone give you a gift from his/her heart.

Be heartless toward someone ...
have someone be heartless toward you.

Make public an indiscretion of someone ...
have someone make public
an indiscretion of yours.

Be inflexible
in your relationship with someone …
have someone be inflexible
in his/her relationship with you.

Be kind to someone …
have someone be kind to you.

Bring a little joy into someone's life …
have someone bring a little joy into your life.

Leer at someone …
have someone leer at you.

Praise someone for her/his good efforts …
have someone praise you for your good efforts.

Pick someone up when he/she is down …
have someone pick you up when you are down.

Provide a shoulder for someone to lean on …
have someone provide a shoulder
for you to lean on.

Give pleasure to someone …
have someone give you pleasure.

Be patient with someone …
have someone be patient with you.

Treat someone poorly …
have someone treat you poorly.

Possess someone …
have someone possess you.

Invade someone's privacy …
have someone invade your privacy.

Help someone be successful at something ...
have someone help you be successful at something.

Spread scandal about someone ...
have someone spread scandal about you.

Share your wisdom with someone ...
have someone share his/her wisdom with you.

Be warmhearted toward someone ...
have someone be warmhearted toward you.

Kiss someone
and tell others whom you have kissed …
have someone kiss you
and tell others about you.

Put the charm on someone
to take advantage of them …
have someone put the charm on you
to take advantage of you.

Intentionally break someone's heart …
have someone intentionally break your heart.

Knowingly give someone a social disease …
have someone knowingly
give you a social disease.

Mistreat someone
because of his/her sexual orientation …
have someone mistreat you
because of your sexual orientation.

Get someone drunk
and take advantage of her/him …
have someone get you drunk
and take advantage of you.

Seduce someone for your pleasure
against his/her desire …
have someone seduce you for his/her pleasure
against your desire.

Unfairly accuse someone of sexual harassment …
be unfairly accused by someone
of sexual harassment.

Rape someone …
be raped by someone.

Treat your significant other as an equal …
have your significant other treat you as an equal.

Demand your spousal right to pleasure
against the desire of your spouse …
have your spouse
demand his/her spousal right for pleasure
against your desire.

Be faithful to your spouse …
have your spouse be faithful to you.

Have an affair with another person
that hurts your spouse …
your spouse will have an affair
that will hurt you.

Break a commitment
you have made to someone …
have someone break a commitment
she/he has made to you.

Henpeck your spouse …
be henpecked by your spouse.

Be a good, loving parent …
be given good, loving parents.

Be disobedient to your parents …
have children who will be disobedient to you.

Neglect your children …
be neglected by your children.

Be an unruly teenager …
have your teenagers be unruly toward you.

Ignore your parents in their old age …
have your children ignore you in your old age.

Father a child
and not take responsibility
for lovingly raising that child …
have someone father you
and not take responsibility
for lovingly raising you.

Mother a child
and not take responsibility
for lovingly raising that child …
have someone mother you
and not take responsibility
for lovingly raising you.

Get a girl/woman pregnant
and leave her with the responsibility
of raising the child alone …
have someone get you pregnant
and leave you with the responsibility
of raising the child alone.

RESPECT

Annoy someone …
be annoyed by someone.

Abuse someone …
be abused by someone.

Abuse many …
be abused by many.

Treat someone in an ignorant manner …
have someone treat you in an ignorant manner.

Have an attitude toward someone ...
someone will have an attitude toward you.

Ask embarrassing questions of someone ...
have someone ask embarrassing questions of you.

Ask embarrassing questions of many ...
have many ask embarrassing questions of you.

Wrongly accuse someone ...
be wrongly accused by someone.

Take advantage of someone …
have someone take advantage of you.

How you take advantage of someone …
is how someone will take advantage of you.

Beat up on someone …
have someone beat up on you.

Betray the confidence
that someone shares with you …
have someone betray the confidence
you share with him/her.

Bore someone to death …
be bored to death by someone.

Borrow something from someone
and forget to return it to her/him …
have someone borrow something from you
and forget to return it to you.

Be intentionally bothersome to someone …
have someone be intentionally bothersome to you.

Bully someone …
have someone bully you.

Blame someone for your mistakes …
have someone blame you for his/her mistakes.

Call someone a name …
have someone call you a name.

Be bullheaded with someone …
have someone be bullheaded with you.

Be brutally candid with someone …
have someone be brutally candid with you.

Be careless toward someone …
have someone be careless toward you.

Be callous toward someone …
have someone be callous toward you.

Be catty toward someone …
have someone be catty toward you.

Be caustic toward someone …
have someone be caustic toward you.

Be chauvinistic toward someone ...
have someone be chauvinistic toward you.

Cheat someone ...
have someone cheat you.

Be uncivil toward someone ...
have someone be uncivil toward you.

Make unfair claims against someone ...
have someone make unfair claims against you.

Treat someone in a classy manner ...
have someone treat you in a classy manner.

Speak coarse language to someone ...
have someone speak coarse language to you.

Be cocky with someone ...
have someone be cocky with you.

Intentionally confuse someone ...
have someone intentionally confuse you.

Be contemptuous toward someone …
have someone be contemptuous toward you.

Corrupt someone …
have someone corrupt you.

Be courteous to someone …
have someone be courteous to you.

Be discourteous to someone …
have someone be discourteous to you.

Give credit where credit is due …
receive credit that is due to you.

Curse someone …
be cursed by someone.

Discriminate against someone
because of the color of her/his skin …
have someone discriminate against you
because of the color of your skin.

Delude someone …
have someone delude you.

Contribute to the delinquency of someone ...
have someone contribute to your delinquency.

Dishonor someone ...
be dishonored by someone.

Intentionally insult someone ...
have someone intentionally insult you.

Be insensitive
to what is offensive to someone ...
have someone be insensitive
to what is offensive to you.

Laugh at someone's faults …
have someone laugh at your faults.

Manipulate someone for your advantage …
have someone manipulate you for her/his advantage.

Be prejudiced toward someone …
have someone be prejudiced toward you.

Be racist toward someone …
have someone be racist toward you.

Be sexist toward someone …
have someone be sexist toward you.

Be understanding of someone …
have someone be understanding of you.

Treat someone poorly because she/he is different …
have someone treat you poorly
because you are different.

Urinate on the toilet seat …
find urine on the seat
when you need to sit.

GROW

Help someone to accomplish a difficult task …
have someone help you
to accomplish a difficult task.

Plant an apple seed …
and, after some years …
and for many years, …
gather many apples.

Bring out the best in someone …
have someone bring out your best.

Be too busy to help anyone in need …
find that everyone will be too busy
to help you
when you are in need.

Help someone to show her/his brilliance …
have someone help you show your brilliance.

Build up someone's self-esteem …
have someone build up your self-esteem.

Cheer up someone
who is down in the dumps …
have someone cheer you up
when you are down in the dumps.

Be conciliatory toward someone …
have someone be conciliatory toward you.

Destroy someone's life
because of your alcohol/drug problem …
have someone destroy your life
because of his/her alcohol/drug problem.

Be demeaning toward someone …
have someone be demeaning toward you.

Demoralize someone …
have someone demoralize you.

Denounce someone …
be denounced by someone.

Disclose personal information about someone …
have someone disclose personal information about you.

Speak discouraging words to someone …
have someone speak discouraging words to you.

Enrich someone …
be enriched by someone.

Be a good example to a younger soul …
have an older soul be a good example to you.

Help someone to excel
in an aspect of his/her life ...
have someone help you excel
in an aspect of your life.

Ease the pain when someone is suffering ...
have someone ease your pain
when you are suffering.

Help someone to gain a freedom ...
have someone help you to gain a freedom.

Free someone from her/his bondage ...
have someone free you from your bondage.

Hold a grudge against someone …
have someone hold a grudge against you.

Hear someone out …
be heard out by someone.

Spread hearsay about someone …
have someone spread hearsay about you.

Humiliate someone …
be humiliated by someone.

Let someone out into heavy traffic ...
have someone let you out into heavy traffic.

Seldom let anyone out into heavy traffic ...
seldom have someone let you out into heavy traffic.

Lie about someone ...
have someone lie about you.

Lie to someone about yourself ...
have someone lie to you about herself/himself.

Label someone unfairly …
have someone label you unfairly.

Take joy in the misfortune of someone …
have someone take joy in your misfortune.

Misinform someone …
have someone misinform you.

Slander someone …
have someone slander you.

The manner in which you help someone …
is the manner in which someone will help you.

The manner in which you hurt someone …
is the manner in which someone will hurt you.

Be sincere in your interactions with someone …
have someone be sincere in his/her interactions with you.

PLAY

Have a loud disturbing party
that inconveniences your neighbors …
be disturbed by a loud party
of your neighbors.

Be a good neighbor to someone …
have someone be a good neighbor to you.

Purposely disgrace someone …
have someone purposely disgrace you.

Intentionally embarrass someone …
have someone intentionally embarrass you.

Be encouraging to someone
who is struggling to learn a skill ...
be encouraged by someone
when you are struggling to learn a skill.

Gloat at someone's loss ...
have someone gloat at your loss.

Be good-natured toward someone ...
have someone be good-natured toward you.

Be a good host to someone ...
have someone be a good host to you.

Be a good guest of someone ...
have someone be a good guest of yours.

Injure someone
because of your reckless driving ...
have someone injure you
because of her/his reckless driving.

Jeer at someone ...
have someone jeer at you.

Play a bad joke on someone ...
have someone play a bad joke on you.

Mock someone …
be mocked by someone.

Be polite to someone …
have someone be polite to you.

Destroy someone's good reputation …
have someone destroy your good reputation.

Speak foul words to someone …
have someone speak foul words to you.

Be gracious toward someone ...
have someone be gracious toward you.

Sock it to someone ...
have someone sock it to you.

Scare someone out of his/her wits ...
have someone scare you out of your wits.

Pull a dirty trick on someone ...
have someone pull a dirty trick on you.

Be vindictive toward someone …
have someone be vindictive toward you.

Run up the score on a sporting opponent
to embarrass them …
have an opponent run up the score on you
to embarrass you.

Totally destroy a sporting opponent …
have an opponent totally destroy you.

Intentionally injure someone …
have someone intentionally injure you.

LEAD

Enlighten someone ...
be enlightened by someone.

Be an inspiration to someone ...
have someone be an inspiration to you.

Be an inspiration to many ...
have many be an inspiration to you.

Pray for someone to be healed ...
have someone pray for you to be healed.

Heckle someone who is speaking …
be heckled by someone while you speak.

Be humble in your dealings with someone …
have someone be humble in his/her dealings with you.

Help someone along in her/his journey …
have someone help you along in your journey.

Falsely incriminate someone …
have someone falsely incriminate you.

Exert undue influence upon someone ...
have someone exert undue influence upon you.

Give someone free instruction ...
have someone give you free instruction.

Interrupt someone when she/he is speaking ...
have someone interrupt you
when you are speaking.

Intentionally misrepresent
what someone has said ...
have someone intentionally misrepresent
what you have said.

Be intransigent with someone …
have someone be intransigent with you.

Help someone to learn
something he/she doesn't get …
have someone help you to learn
something you don't get.

Listen thoughtfully
to someone who is speaking …
have someone listen thoughtfully to you
when you are speaking.

Show your loyalty to someone …
have someone show her/his loyalty to you.

Be a good mentor to someone …
have someone be a good mentor to you.

Be merciful toward someone …
have someone be merciful toward you.

Misrepresent the teachings of someone …
have someone misrepresent your teachings.

Motivate someone to do her/his best …
have someone motivate you to do your best.

Be open-minded with someone ...
have someone be open-minded with you.

Be disrespectful toward someone ...
have someone be disrespectful toward you.

Be rude toward someone ...
have someone be rude toward you.

Treat someone ruthlessly ...
have someone treat you ruthlessly.

Support someone …
have someone support you.

Treat someone as a second-class person …
have someone treat you as a second-class person.

Suppress someone
from expressing his/her thoughts …
have someone suppress you
from expressing your thoughts.

Say something thoughtful to someone …
have someone say something thoughtful to you.

Speak comforting words to someone ...
have someone speak comforting words to you.

Speak highly of someone ...
have someone speak highly of you.

Tutor someone ...
be tutored by someone.

Be tolerant of someone
of lesser understanding ...
have someone be tolerant
of your lack of understanding.

Oppress someone …
be oppressed by someone.

Enslave those who have given you
the responsibility to govern them …
be enslaved by those
to whom you have given
the responsibility to govern you.

Rule with an iron hand over people …
be ruled over with an iron hand
by other people.

Torture someone …
be tortured by someone.

Be accepting of the different beliefs of someone ...
have someone be accepting of your different beliefs.

Ridicule the spiritual beliefs of someone ...
have someone ridicule your spiritual beliefs.

Deny someone the right to her/his beliefs ...
have someone deny you the right to your beliefs.

Give someone his/her free-will choice
to grow in his/her own way ...
have someone give you the free-will choice
to grow in your own way.

Impose your spiritual beliefs
upon someone ...
have someone impose her/his spiritual beliefs
upon you.

Condemn someone to hell ...
have someone condemn you to hell.

Accuse someone of being possessed by the devil ...
have someone accuse you of being possessed
by the devil.

Label someone a heathen ...
be labeled a heathen by someone.

Discriminate against someone
for any reason
because of his/her spiritual beliefs …
have someone discriminate against you
because of your spiritual beliefs.

Accuse someone of being a heretic …
have someone accuse you of being a heretic.

Indoctrinate someone with false teachings
to control her/him …
have someone indoctrinate you with false teachings
to control you.

WORK

Compliment someone for her/his good efforts …
have someone compliment you for your good efforts.

Compliment many people
for their good efforts …
have many people compliment you
for your good efforts.

Unfairly criticize someone …
have someone unfairly criticize you.

Dig into someone's personal life
and make it public …
have someone dig into your personal life
and make it public.

Tell someone a distasteful joke/story ...
have someone tell you a distasteful joke/story.

Nastily expose the shortcomings of someone ...
have someone nastily expose your shortcomings.

Be envious of someone's success at work ...
have someone be envious of your success at work.

Exploit someone ...
be exploited by someone.

Excuse the shortcomings of someone ...
have someone excuse your shortcomings.

Extort money from someone ...
have someone extort money from you.

Extort money from many ...
have many extort money from you.

Flaunt your success to someone ...
have someone flaunt his/her success to you.

Do a flimsy job for someone ...
have someone do a flimsy job for you.

Tell someone a fib ...
have someone tell you a fib.

Frame someone for something
she/he did not do ...
have someone frame you
for something you did not do.

Be fraudulent in your dealings with someone ...
have someone be fraudulent
in his/her dealings with you.

Spread gossip about someone …
have someone spread gossip about you.

Express your gratitude to someone …
have someone express her/his gratitude to you.

Be disruptive to someone giving an address …
have someone be disruptive
when you give an address.

Second-guess someone …
have someone second-guess you.

Be heavy-handed
in your dealings with someone …
have someone be heavy-handed
in her/his dealings with you.

Intentionally inconvenience someone …
have someone intentionally inconvenience you.

Be a hindrance to someone on his/her job …
have someone be a hindrance to you
on your job.

Hoodwink someone …
be hoodwinked by someone.

Be hotheaded toward someone …
have someone be hotheaded toward you.

Praise someone for a job well done …
have someone praise you for a job well done.

Speak loudly in public and annoy someone …
have someone speak loudly in public and annoy you.

Manufacture an untrue story about someone …
have someone manufacture
an untrue story about you.

Meddle in the affairs of someone …
have someone meddle in your affairs.

Maliciously offend someone …
have someone maliciously offend you.

Ask someone a pointed question
that puts them on the spot publicly …
have someone ask you a pointed question
that puts you on the spot publicly.

Pry into someone's personal affairs …
have someone pry into your personal affairs.

Fail to repay your debt to someone …
have someone fail to repay her/his debt to you.

Sabotage someone's plans …
have someone sabotage your plans.

Speak sarcastically to someone …
have someone speak sarcastically to you.

Swindle someone …
have someone swindle you.

How you treat someone …
is how someone will treat you.

Make someone's job a little easier …
have someone make your job a little easier.

Do an excellent job for your employer …
have your employees do an excellent job for you.

Do a sloppy job for someone …
have someone do a sloppy job for you.

Charge someone an excessive fee
for your services ...
have someone charge you
an excessive fee for his/her services.

Unfairly compensate someone for her/his services ...
have someone unfairly compensate you
for your services.

Palm off on someone a poor product ...
have someone palm off on you
a poor product.

Overcharge someone for a product ...
have someone overcharge you for a product.

Defraud a customer ...
be defrauded as a customer.

Make someone look good in her/his job ...
have someone make you look good
in your job.

Make someone look bad in his/her job ...
have someone make you look bad
in your job.

Disappoint someone by doing a poor job ...
have someone disappoint you
by doing a poor job for you.

Knowingly sell a "lemon" to someone ...
have someone knowingly sell you a "lemon."

Employ someone for minimum wage
while you bask in the luxury
of your exorbitant profits ...
be employed by someone for minimum wage
while she/he basks in the luxury
of her/his exorbitant profits.

Entice someone to do something
for your personal profit ...
have someone entice you to do something
for his/her personal profit.

Intentionally give someone erroneous information
that causes him/her a loss
or brings harm to him/her ...
have someone intentionally give you erroneous information
that causes you a loss
or brings harm to you.

Pull a shady deal on someone ...
have someone pull a shady deal on you.

Reward someone for doing a good job …
be rewarded by someone for doing a good job.

Reward many for doing a good job …
be rewarded by many for doing a good job.

Annihilate a business competitor …
have a business competitor annihilate you.

Sell someone a good product at a reasonable price …
have someone sell you a good product
at a reasonable price.

Don't hire someone
because of his/her spiritual beliefs …
have someone not hire you
because of your spiritual beliefs.

CONFLICT

Abduct someone's child …
have someone abduct your child.

Bear false witness against someone …
have someone bear false witness against you.

Tell half-truths about someone …
have someone tell half-truths about you.

Coerce someone into doing something
against her/his will …
have someone coerce you into doing something
against your will.

Conspire to harm someone …
have someone conspire to harm you.

Knowingly contradict the truth
to someone …
have someone knowingly contradict the truth
to you.

Cut someone's throat …
have someone cut your throat.

Give false evidence against someone …
have someone give false evidence against you.

Enslave someone physically …
have someone enslave you physically.

Enslave someone economically …
have someone enslave you economically.

Enslave someone mentally …
have someone enslave you mentally.

Intentionally hurt someone …
have someone intentionally hurt you.

Hate someone …
be hated by someone.

Break into someone's home …
have someone break into your home.

How you harm someone …
is how someone will harm you.

Be a headache to someone ...
have someone be a headache to you.

Speak harshly to someone ...
have someone speak harshly to you.

Be mean toward someone ...
have someone be mean toward you.

Be menacing toward someone …
have someone be menacing toward you.

Intentionally maim someone …
have someone intentionally maim you.

Be unmerciful toward someone …
have someone be unmerciful toward you.

Plot against someone …
have someone plot against you.

Poison someone …
be poisoned by someone.

Persecute someone …
be persecuted by someone.

Speak profane words to someone …
have someone speak profane words to you.

Punch someone out …
have someone punch you out.

Screw someone …
be screwed by someone.

Spread personal information about someone …
have someone spread personal information
about you.

Stab someone in the back …
have someone stab you in the back.

Threaten to kill someone …
have someone threaten to kill you.

Terrify someone ...
be terrified by someone.

Torment someone ...
be tormented by someone.

Knowingly give bad advice to someone ...
have someone knowingly give you bad advice.

Wrongly accuse someone of something
that sends him/her to prison ...
have someone wrongly accuse you of something
that sends you to prison.

Invade the homeland of a people …
have other people invade your homeland.

Take someone hostage …
have someone take you hostage.

Repress a people …
be repressed by other people.

War against another country …
have another country war against you.

Expel someone from her/his home ...
be expelled from your home by someone.

Force people from their village ...
be forced from your village by other people.

Remove people from their homeland ...
be removed from your homeland
by other people.

Pillage and plunder a people
as you war upon them ...
have people pillage and plunder you in war.

CHARITY

Feed a hungry person ...
have a person feed you
when you are hungry.

Feed many hungry people ...
have many people feed you
when you are hungry.

Be greedy ...
in time,
be a pauper.

Be generous to those
who suffer from a natural disaster ...
have others be generous
when you suffer from a natural disaster.

Hoard when others have need ...
have need while others hoard.

Impoverish someone ...
be impoverished by someone.

Steal from someone ...
be stolen from by someone.

Give shelter to someone …
have someone give shelter to you.

Share your secrets of success with someone …
have someone share her/his secrets of success
with you.

Be stingy toward people …
in time,
have people be stingy toward you.

Talk about someone behind her/his back …
have someone talk about you
behind your back.

Give to someone who feeds you spiritually …
have someone give to you
when you feed her/him spiritually.

Be generous …
receive generously.

What you give …
is what you get.

Never give …
never get.

Give of your time to help those in need ...
have others give of their time
when you are in need.

Give a little to someone in need ...
receive a little when you are in need.

Give much to those in need ...
receive much when you are in need.

Give a little money ...
receive a little money.

Give much money ...
receive much money.

Give nothing ...
receive nothing.

SUMMMARY

What you plant …
is what you harvest.

The more that you plant …
the more that you will harvest.

Plant nothing …
harvest nothing.

Plant a vegetable garden …
harvest vegetables.

Plant a flower garden …
gather flowers.

Don't plant a garden …
don't harvest.

What you do to someone ...
someone will do to you.

What you do for someone ...
someone will do for you.

Do wrong to someone ...
have someone do wrong to you.

Do nothing to help anyone ...
have no one do anything to help you.

The earlier in your life
that you do something to someone
or for someone ...
the earlier in your life
that someone will do something
to or for you.

If you don't do for someone
what you could have done ...
others will not do for you
what they could have done.

Do unto others ...
as you would have others do unto you.

AS you do unto others ...
IT WILL be done unto you.

We have chosen our happiness and our pains ...
by our actions in earlier times.

We are choosing our future experiences ...
by our current actions.

The first shall be last ...
and the last shall be first.

Give to life the best you can ...
and the best will come back to you.

Time heals all wounds.
Time wounds all heels.

The actions of every soul
result in like and equal actions
returning unfailingly to that soul.

Whatever you want
to come into your life ...
you must first be that for someone ...
you must first do that for someone ...
you must first give that to someone.

Every soul creates its own future.
What that soul has done
in its unbelieving past,
it must unfailingly experience in the future.

Because a soul disbelieves something ...
does not stop that something from happening.

The grass is green …
where you make it green.

Think it ...
Say it ...
Do it ...
Be it ...
Give it ...
HAVE IT!!!

What goes around ...
comes around.

At the point in time
that a soul GETS IT ...
and chooses to do good in all manners
rather than wrong in any manner,
that soul is on the path to freedom ...
and a future filled with joy and prosperity.

The thing that has been
is the thing that shall be ...
and the thing that is done
is that which shall be done ...
There is nothing new under the sun.

—Solomon

The laws sometimes seem to sleep …
but never die.

—Ancient Chinese proverb

In the Game of Life,
there is only one set of rules.
Learn them ...
live them ...
then you'll enjoy the Game.

That ABSOLUTE TRUTH
is not commonly known …
does not stop ABSOLUTE TRUTH
from existing …
nor stop ABSOLUTE TRUTH
from being ABSOLUTELY TRUE.

One who knows ABSOLUTE TRUTH …
will not insist that you accept ABSOLUTE TRUTH
as being ABSOLUTELY TRUE.

GET IT YET?

MY PERSONAL RULES

LaVergne, TN USA
25 November 2009

165269LV00004B/9/P